DOG ON A LOG™
Let's GO! Books
Step 1

DOG ON A LOG Books
Tucson, Arizona

Public Domain images from
www.clker.com

ISBN: 978-1949471069

www.dogonalogbooks.com

FIVE
LET'S GO!
BOOKS
1

A companion to
FIVE CHAPTER BOOKS 1

DOG ON A LOG Let's GO! Books
Step 1

By Pamela Brookes

Download DOG ON A LOG printable gameboards, games, flashcards, and other activities at:
www.dogonalogbooks.com/printables.

Parents and Teachers:
Receive email notifications of new books and printables. Sign up at:
www.dogonalogbooks.com/subscribe

Table of Contents

DOG ON A LOG
Parent and Teacher Guides

General information
on Dyslexia and
Struggling Readers

The Author's Routine
for Teaching Reading

Book 1. *Teaching a Struggling Reader: One Mom's Experience with Dyslexia*

Book 2. *How to Use Decodable Books to Teach Reading*

Available for free from many online booksellers or read at:
www.dogonalogbooks.com/free

THE DOG
ON THE LOG

The dog is on a log.

His kid is Jan.

"Let us go to the dam," Jan says.

Jan is wet.

Tup does not like to get wet.

Jan is wet. She is OK.

Tup can see a fish.

Hop, hop, hop, to the fish.

This is fun!

A pup.

A dog.

Sight Words used in
"THE DOG ON THE LOG"

a, does, go, his, is, like, OK, says, see, she, the, to

Approximately 50 total words

THE PIG HAT

Pam is a big pig.

Sam got a hat.

Sam set the hat on the pig.

Sam and Pam go for a jog. They jog to the pig shop.

Pam can not go in the pig shop.

Pam has to sit in the shop gal's hot rod.

It is a red hot rod.

Pam has a pig yum.

PIG
YUM

Sight Words used in "The Pig Hat"

a, and, for, go, has, is, says, she, the, they, to

Approximately 55 total words

CHAD THE CAT

Liz has a cat. Her cat is Chad.

Chad goes bam on the rug.

"The vet can fix him up," Mom says.

They get in the
van.

They go to see the
vet.

"I can fix him up," the vet says.

"You can sit when I fix him up," the vet says.

"I did fix up Chad. He can go with you," the vet says.

Chad is Liz's pal.

Sight Words used in "CHAD THE CAT"

a, go, goes, has, he, her, is, says, see, the, they, to, you

Approximately 70 total words

ZIP THE BUG

Zip the bug had a nap in his mug.

Zip's mug is in the hot sun. Hop, hop, hop. He is not in his mug.

Zip's pal, Tag, is on the rug. "Let us go get Jot," Zip says.

Zip and Tag hop on the rug. The sun is hot.

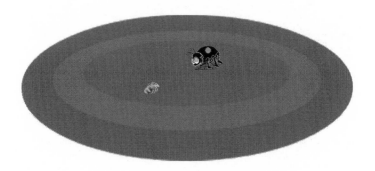

They hop to the cat dish. They do not see the cat.

The cat is bad if you are a bug.

They see a web. A web is bad if you are a bug.

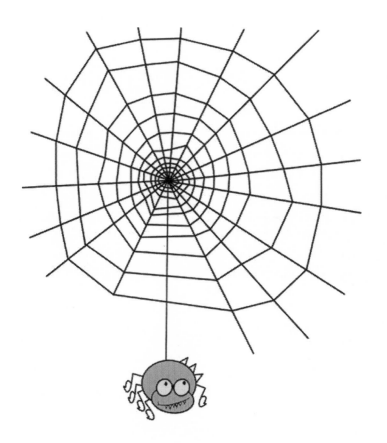

They see a log. Jot is on the log.

Zip, Tag, and Jot get on the log. It is fun.

Sight Words used in "ZIP THE BUG"

a, and, are, do, go, he, his, is, says, see, the, they, to, you

Approximately 105 total words

THE FISH
AND THE PIG

Val is a fish. Her pal Pam does not like to get wet.

"You do not like to get wet. Can the man get us a jug I can sit in?" the fish says.

The pig goes to the man. He has on Pam's hat.

The man has a jug.

Pam sees the jug.

She has the jug.

"Here, get in the jug," Pam says.

The fish can be with her pal.

"Let me see if I have a big jug for the fish," the man says.

The fish has a pal.

Her pal is not wet.

Sight Words used in
"THE FISH AND THE PIG"

a, and, be, do, does, for, goes, has, have, he, her, here, I, is, like, me, says, see, sees, she, the, to, you

Approximately 100 total words

KEYWORDS

Alphabet

Aa	Bb
apple	bat
Cc	Dd
cat	dog

Ee

Ed

Ff

fun

Gg

game

Hh

hat

Ii

itch

Jj

jug

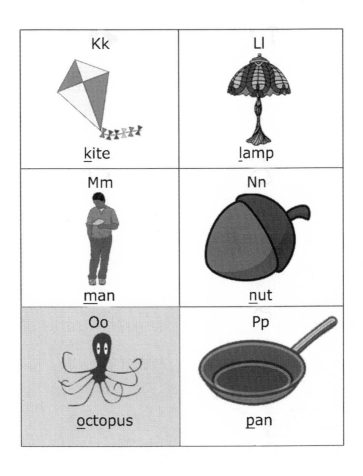

Kk	Ll
kite	lamp
Mm	Nn
man	nut
Oo	Pp
octopus	pan

Qu qu	Rr
<u>qu</u>een	<u>r</u>at
Ss	Tt
<u>s</u>nake	<u>t</u>op
Uu	Vv
<u>u</u>p	<u>v</u>an

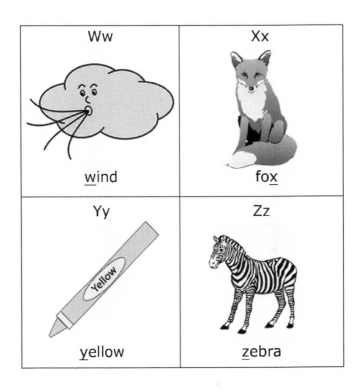

Ww	Xx
<u>w</u>ind	fo<u>x</u>
Yy	Zz
<u>y</u>ellow	<u>z</u>ebra

Digraphs

ch	sh
chin	ship
th	th
thumb	mother
wh	-ck
whistle	sock

DOG ON A LOG Books
Phonics Progression

DOG ON A LOG Pup Books
Book 1
Phonological/Phonemic Awareness:
- Words
- Rhyming
- Syllables, identification, blending, segmenting
- Identifying individual letter sounds

Books 2-3
Phonemic Awareness/Phonics
- Consonants, primary sounds
- Short vowels
- Blending
- Introduction to sight words

DOG ON A LOG Let's GO! and Chapter Books

Step 1
- Consonants, primary sounds
- Short vowels
- Digraphs: ch, sh, th, wh, ck
- 2 and 3 sound words
- Possessive 's

Step 2
- Bonus letters (f, l, s, z after short vowel)
- "all"
- –s suffix

Step 3
- Letter Buddies: ang, ing, ong, ung, ank, ink, onk, unk

Step 4
- Consonant blends to make 4 sound words
- 3 and 4 sound words ending in –lk, -sk

Step 5
- Digraph blend –nch to make 3 and 4 sound words
- Silent e, including "-ke"

Step 6
- Exception words containing: ild, old, olt, ind, ost

Step 7
- 5 sounds in a closed syllable word plus suffix -s (crunch, slumps)
- 3 letter blends and up to 6 sounds in a closed syllable word (script, spring)

Step 8

- Two-syllable words with 2 closed syllables, not blends (sunset, chicken, unlock)

Step 9

- Two-syllable words with all previously introduced sounds including blends, exception words, and silent "e" (blacksmith, kindness, inside)
- Vowel digraphs: ai, ay, ea, ee, ie, oa, oe (rain, play, beach, tree, pie, boat, toe)

WATCH FOR MORE STEPS COMING SOON

Let's GO! Books have less text

Chapter Books are longer

DOG ON A LOG Books
Sight Word Progression

DOG ON A LOG Pup Books
a, does, go, has, her is, of, says, the, to

DOG ON A LOG Let's GO! and Chapter Books

Step 1
a, and, are, be, does, go, goes, has, he, her, his, into, is, like, my, of, OK, says, see, she, the, they, to, want, you

Step 2
could, do, eggs, for, from, have, here, I, likes, me, nest, onto, or, puts, said, say, sees, should, wants, was, we, what, would, your

Step 3
as, Mr., Mrs., no, put, their, there, where

Step 4
push, saw

Step 5
come, comes, egg, pull, pulls, talk, walk, walks

Step 6
Ms., so, some, talks

Step 7
Hmmm, our, out, Pop E., TV

Step 8
Dr., friend, full, hi, island, people, please

More DOG ON A LOG Books

Free E-book or PDF Bookfold

DOG ON A LOG Parent and Teacher Guides

Book 1
- Teaching a Struggling Reader: One Mom's Experience with Dyslexia **(also Paperback)**

Book 2
- How to Use Decodable Books to Teach Reading

Paperback or E-book
DOG ON A LOG Pup Books

Book 1
- Before the Squiggle Code (A Roadmap to Reading)

Books 2-3
- The Squiggle Code (Letters Make Words)
- Kids' Squiggles (Letters Make Words)

DOG ON A LOG Let's GO! and Chapter Books

Step 1
- The Dog on the Log
- The Pig Hat
- Chad the Cat
- Zip the Bug
- The Fish and the Pig

Step 2
- Mud on the Path
- The Red Hen
- The Hat and Bug Shop
- Babs the 'Bot
- The Cub

Step 3
- Mr. Bing has Hen Dots
- The Junk Lot Cat
- Bonk Punk Hot Rod
- The Ship with Wings
- The Sub in the Fish Tank

Step 4
- The Push Truck
- The Sand Hill
- Lil Tilt and Mr. Ling
- Musk Ox in the Tub
- The Trip to the Pond
-

Step 5
- Bake a Cake
- The Crane at the Cave
- Ride a Bike
- Crane or Crane?
- The Swing Gate

Step 6
- The Colt
- The Gold Bolt
- Hide in the Blinds
- The Stone Child
- Tolt the Kind Cat

Step 7
- Quest for A Grump Grunt
- The Blimp
- The Spring in the Lane
- Stamp for a Note
- Stripes and Splats

Step 8
- Anvil and Magnet
- The Mascot
- Kevin's Rabbit Hole
- The Humbug Vet and Medic Shop
- Chickens in the Attic

All chapter books can be purchased individually or with all the same-step books in one volume.

Steps 1-5 can be bought as Let's GO! Books which are less text companions to the chapter books.

All titles are available as chapter books.

WATCH FOR MORE BOOKS COMING SOON

How You Can Help

Parents often worry that their child (or even adult learner) is not going to learn to read. Hearing other people's successes (especially when they struggled) can give worried parents or teachers hope. I would encourage others to share their experiences with products you've used by posting reviews at your favorite bookseller(s) stating how your child benefitted from those books or materials (whether it was DOG ON A LOG Books or another book or product.) This will help other parents and teachers know which products they should consider using. More than that, hearing your successes could truly help another family feel hopeful. It's amazing that something as seemingly small as a review can ease someone's concerns.

Made in the USA
Middletown, DE
30 January 2020